Super Dogs

Contents

Written by Swapna Haddow

Collins

Super dogs

Dogs are super smart. They have super noses and super ears. This makes them true superstars.

In this book you will meet dogs with astonishing talents.

Rescue dogs

A dog's super nose can help to rescue people.

Panuco has saved lots of people using his nose.

Fact!
A uniform of boots and a shield protects Panuco.

Dogs can smell a trapped or wounded person and lead a rescue crew to them.

In 1945, this dog, named Rip, got a medal for rescuing people in the **Blitz**.

Dogs don't just rescue humans.

This **former** stray dog has sniffed out and rescued hundreds of lost kittens.

Fact!

This dog rescued a duckling from the reeds in a pond!

Dogs on the job

Dogs can be trained to
help blind people.

This dog should help people when its **harness** is on. When its harness is off, it can play!

Mist is a sheepdog. She helps farmers keep their animals safe on the farm by herding them into groups.

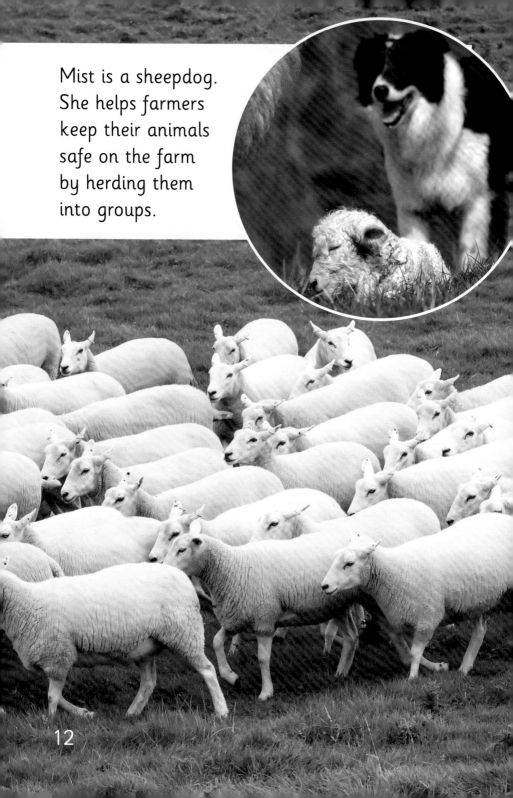

Fact!
One sheepdog can herd a group of 100 sheep.

Sled dogs are quick. They are super at pulling sleds.

Togo's crew carried an important drug on their sled.

Togo

Fact!
Sled dogs need lots of food!

Sporting dogs

Super dogs are super quick and alert. This makes them good at sport.

Abbie set a new record for the longest wave surfed by a dog!

Few people would disagree that Norman is a super dog!

18

He rides his scooter down the street.

Fact!
Norman holds the record
for the quickest dog on
a scooter!

Some dogs like to skip with their humans.

Little dogs like this one don't need a rope to skip!
It uses its human's arms.

Dogs in orbit

Dogs have been in **orbit**!
How super is that?

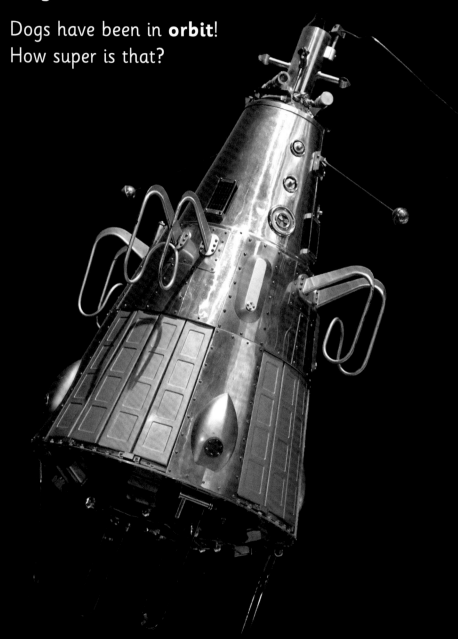

Laika the dog went into orbit. She had a super suit!

Fact!
Laika was once a stray dog.

Boss dogs

Duke was not an astro dog but he *was* in
the top spot ...

He was chosen to be the leader of his town!

Fact!
Humans **voted** for Duke!

Dogs that clean up

There are dogs that are just super
at being super.

Have you met a super dog?

Glossary

Blitz a term used for the attacks on the UK by planes between 1940 and 1941

former used to be

harness straps attached to a dog

orbit travel in the air near a planet

voted when people chose a person to do a job

Index

Super dogs, super skills

rescue dogs

dogs on the job

sporting dogs

dogs in orbit

boss dogs

dogs that clean up

After reading

Letters and Sounds: Phase 5

Word count: 394

Focus phonemes: /ai/ ay, a-e, ey /ee/ ie, ea /igh/ i-e, i /oa/ o, o-e /oo/ ue, ui, ew, ou, u, oul, u-e

Common exception words: of, the, into, by, pulling, he, she, be, have, little, when, their, people, there, out, was, some, to, are, one, once

Curriculum links: Science: Animals, including humans

National Curriculum learning objectives: Reading/word reading: apply phonic knowledge and skills as the route to decode words; read accurately by blending sounds in unfamiliar words containing GPCs that have been taught; Reading/comprehension (KS2): understand what they read, in books they can read independently, by checking that the text makes sense to them, discussing their understanding and explaining the meaning of words in context; identifying main ideas drawn from more than one paragraph and summarising these

Developing fluency

- Take it in turns to read a page with your child, ensuring they read labels and fact boxes too.
- Encourage your child to read with expression, adding emphasis to 'Fact!' and sentences that end in an exclamation mark.

Phonic practice

- Focus on words with /oo/ sounds. Ask your child to sound out and blend the following:
  scooter   rescue   crew   suit   should
- For each of the above, can they match the word with the same /oo/ spelling?
  would   cue   fruit   food   chew

Extending vocabulary

- Look together at each of the following words in context and discuss their meaning.
  page 2: smart (e.g. *clever*)   page 12: safe (e.g. *secure, unharmed*)
  page 20: skip (e.g. *jump, hop*)
- Challenge your child to think of a different meaning for each word.
  (e.g. smart – *well-dressed, neat*; safe – *cash box*; skip – *miss out, leave out*)